Griff
and the
Griffin

Meg Harper

OXFORD
UNIVERSITY PRESS

Great Clarendon Street, Oxford, OX2 6DP,
United Kingdom

Oxford University Press is a department of the University of Oxford.
It furthers the University's objective of excellence in research, scholarship,
and education by publishing worldwide. Oxford is a registered trade mark of
Oxford University Press in the UK and in certain other countries

Text © Meg Harper 2017

Illustrations © Graham Howells 2017

The moral rights of the author have been asserted

First published 2017

British Library Cataloguing in Publication Data
Data available

978-0-19-837769-6

1 3 5 7 9 10 8 6 4 2

Paper used in the production of this book is a natural, recyclable product
made from wood grown in sustainable forests. The manufacturing process
conforms to the environmental regulations of the country of origin.

Printed in China by Leo Paper Products Ltd.

Contents

Chapter 1
An Extra Egg

It was a horrible wet day when Mum sent Griff Griffiths down to the henhouse to collect the eggs. He felt cold and grumpy.

The hens huddled together and clucked at Griff. They looked grumpy too.

"Sorry, but Mum wants your eggs," said Griff. "Don't look like that."

Griff Griffith's life was about to change forever. He didn't know this, of course. But he did know that there were four eggs instead of three in the nesting box. And one of them was dark green.

"Wow!" said Griff. "Did one of you lay that?"

The hens ignored him and carried on pecking the grass.

Griff picked up the green egg carefully. It was making a noise. A noise a bit like ticking and not quite like scratching.

Griff stood in the rain and watched as a thin crack appeared in the shell. It grew bigger and bigger. Griff could hardly breathe for excitement. Something was hatching out of the dark green egg!

First, a sharp beak appeared. Then two bright, beady eyes peeped out. And then some curly claws pulled the shell apart. Griff stared down at the strangest creature he had ever seen in his life. But then he had an even bigger shock.

"Hello," croaked the creature, cocking its head on one side. "I'm Hexxa and I'm a griffin. Who and what are you?"

Griff didn't drop the creature. He didn't jump in the air and scream. He was a quick thinker and he read a lot. He knew what a griffin was: a cross between an eagle and a lion. This one was very small but it was definitely a griffin.

"I'm Griff Griffiths and I'm a boy," said Griff. "Err … I don't suppose you know where you've come from? Or why you're here?"

"No," said Hexxa the griffin. "But I do know I'm hungry."

"Really?" said Griff. "What do griffins like to eat?"

"Meat," said Hexxa at once. "Are boys meat?"

"No," said Griff. "Definitely not." This was a lie, of course, but Griff thought the truth might be dangerous.

Just then, Mum opened the back door.

"It's time to go to school," she shouted. "Hurry up!"

Griff's mind was a whirl. Should he leave the griffin or take it to school with him? No contest. He shoved Hexxa in his pocket and ran up the garden. He thrust the eggs into his mum's hands.

Three minutes later, he was sitting in the car. He put his hand in his pocket.

"Yeeooow!" he yelled. Hexxa had
dug her beak into his finger. "Hey, stop
that!" he said.

Mum jumped into the car and they
roared off.

"Yeoow!" shrieked Griff again, and he
leaped in the air.

The car swerved.

"What's up with you?" Mum demanded.

"Something's digging into my leg," said Griff.

"Well, there's no need to make such a noise! I nearly had an accident!"

"Sorry, Mum," said Griff. He just hoped Hexxa didn't do it again!

She did.

"Yeoww!" Griff shrieked.

Mum slammed on the brakes. She turned to Griff.

"Get out and walk to school," she said. "I don't know why you're making those silly noises but I haven't got time to find out! I have a very important meeting at work."

"But Mum … " said Griff.

"But nothing," said his mum. "Your school is a five-minute walk away. It's stopped raining. Now go!"

Griff did as he was told.

"Sorry, Mum. Bye," he said.

Mum watched Griff go. She saw him leap in the air and slap his thigh. What *was* the matter with him? She shook her head and drove on.

Chapter 2
Enter Constance
Amelia Grisold

"Stop it, Hexxa!" growled Griff, as the car roared away. "You're hurting me!"

Hexxa stuck her head out of his pocket. "I'm hungry," she said. "And you smell yummy!"

She ducked back down into his pocket.

"Yeoww!" shouted Griff.

He dragged Hexxa out and glared into her beady eyes.

"Now listen up, Hexxa," he said. "I am NOT breakfast!"

"Why not?" said Hexxa. "You wouldn't miss a bit!"

Griff frowned. Some mean kids called him names because of his size. He didn't need a griffin that joined in. "For the last time," he snapped, "boys are NOT food!"

"Then what is?" whined Hexxa.

"I'll think of something," said Griff.
"Just give me some time!"

But Hexxa burst out of Griff's hands.
She flew across the road. A butcher
was unloading his van. Hexxa started
pecking at a huge joint of meat!

"Get off!" bellowed the butcher,
swiping at her. "Dirty starlings!"

But Hexxa just carried on pecking.

Griff watched in horror. He couldn't dash across the road – the traffic was far too busy.

The butcher ran inside his shop.

"Hexxa!" Griff shouted. "Come back! Leave it alone! Stop!"

The butcher had come back with a broom.

"Dirty starlings!" he yelled again and swung the broom at Hexxa.

Griff spotted a gap in the traffic and quickly crossed the road. He launched himself at Hexxa and landed – splat! – right on top of her.

The butcher staggered backwards and lost his balance. Smash! The broom went straight through the shop window!

Griff didn't wait to see what the butcher would do. He grabbed Hexxa, scrambled to his feet and ran away as fast as he could. He caught up with a gang of kids from his school.

"Hey Griff! What are *you* doing here?" It was Todd, Griff's best friend.

"I was messing about in the car so Mum made me walk," said Griff. He shoved Hexxa in his pocket quickly.

But Todd never missed anything.

"What are you hiding?" he said. "Show me!"

Griff hesitated. He wasn't sure he wanted to share Hexxa but he could see that he was going to need Todd's help. Carefully, he got Hexxa out of his pocket.

"What's that?" demanded Todd. "A baby eagle?"

Hexxa let out a shriek. "An eagle?" she squawked. "How dare you?"

Todd turned pale. "It sp … sp … oke," he gibbered. "Griff … wh … where did you get that thing?"

"It hatched out of an egg in our henhouse this morning," said Griff.

"But it's a *griffin*!" said Todd. "Griffins aren't real!"

"Not real!" shrieked Hexxa, and she flew straight for Todd's head!

"Yikes! Do something, Griff!" shouted Todd. "Aaaagh! It pecked my ear!"

Other children were beginning to look. Griff was frantic.

"What's that?" asked a little girl with ginger plaits.

"It's my pet parrot," Griff said. "It's got a very bad temper."

"Why have you brought it to school then?" she demanded.

"For a project," he said. "Now go away – you're annoying her."

"No I'm not," said the little girl. "If you put a blanket over her, she'll go to sleep."

"I haven't got a blanket!" shouted
Griff.

"Aaaagh, it's pulling my hair out!"
shrieked Todd.

The little girl rolled her eyes. "Lie
down!" she yelled.

"What?" said Todd.

"Just do as I say."

Todd lay on the floor. The little girl
tore off her cardigan and threw it over
Todd's head.

"Grab the griffin!" she shouted at
Griff. "Quickly!"

Griff was getting fed up with this
little girl, but he hadn't got any better
ideas so he did as she said.

"Has it gone?" gasped Todd, sitting up.

"Err … 'fraid not," said Griff, "but
I've got her safely wrapped up." He glared
at the little girl. "How do you know she's
a griffin?"

"Because I'm not stupid!" said the girl.

At that moment, Hexxa jabbed Griff's

hand. "Aaaagh!" he yelled.

"Let me out!" Hexxa squawked. "It's dark and my tummy hurts."

"Serves you right!" said Griff grumpily, but he unwrapped her.

Hexxa stared at the little girl. "I'm Hexxa," she said. "Who are you?"

"I'm Constance Amelia Grisold," said the little girl. "Pleased to meet you." She put out a finger.

"Careful!" said Griff.

Constance stroked Hexxa gently.

"Nice," said Hexxa sleepily. "Very nice. I might just have a little na … p." She tucked her head under her wing.

"There," said Constance. "She's only a baby. She needs a sleep. Now come on or we'll be late for school."

"But what am I going to do with Hexxa?" said Griff. "She's always hungry!"

Constance opened her lunchbox.

"You can have this," she said and pulled out a sandwich. "It's corned beef. Yuk. But Hexxa might like it. See you later!"

And she ran off.

"Come on," said Griff. "We'd better hurry!"

"Don't wake up Hexxa, whatever you do!" said Todd.

Griff looked down at the feathery bundle in his hands. Hexxa looked so sweet and harmless. What a joke!

Everyone was marching into assembly when Griff and Todd arrived at school. They slid into their places just as Mrs Herbert, the head teacher, walked in. Following her was a police officer!

"Good morning, everyone," said Mrs Herbert briskly. "As you can see, we have a visitor. PC Ahmad tells me that a strange bird attacked the local butcher this morning – and a boy from our school rescued it. So the question is, who was that boy?"

"Yikes," thought Griff. "What am I going to do now?" He glanced at Todd, but Todd just shrugged.

"Errr …" said Griff. He began to put up his hand.

"Griff Griffiths," said Mrs Herbert, sounding very surprised. "Was it *you*?"

At that very moment, Hexxa woke up and gave Griff a nasty jab in his thigh. Griff leaped in the air.

"Er … sorry, Mrs Herbert," he gasped. What could he say? "Err … I've got to go to the toilet – right now!"

Chapter 3
Poor Miss Tracey!

The whole school turned to gape at Griff. He sprinted down the corridor, leaping in the air every few paces.

"Griff Griffiths, stop running!" shouted the school secretary.

"Sorry!" he called back, skidding into the boys' toilets. He locked himself into a cubicle. Then he yanked Hexxa out of his pocket.

"I'm hungr—"

"Stop that!" hissed Griff. "Just be quiet and eat this!" He pulled out Constance's sandwich.

"Yummy," said Hexxa. "Scrummy."

"Phew!" said Griff. He leaned against the door. "Think really fast!" he told himself.

"Listen, Hexxa," he said. "I don't know why you're here but I want to be friends. So you can't keep pecking me!"

"But it's nasty in your pocket!" said Hexxa. "And I'm hungry!"

"I know," said Griff, "but I need some time to sort things out!"

"Griff Griffiths? Are you all right?" It was Miss Tracey, a teaching assistant.

"Shh, Hexxa!" hissed Griff.

"Not really," he called. "I think I need to go home!"

"The police officer wants to see you," said Miss Tracey.

"But I don't feel very well," said Griff feebly.

"That's all right," said Miss Tracey. "The police officer can wait."

"Now look at the mess you've got me into," Griff hissed at Hexxa.

Hexxa tossed her head.

"What's that, Griff?" asked Miss Tracey.

"Oh, nothing," said Griff. "Must be the pipes gurgling."

"I'll wait," said Miss Tracey. "Tell me when you feel better."

Griff thought frantically. What was he going to do? Then he heard a surprisingly welcome voice.

"Excuse me," said Constance. "There's a flood in the girls' toilets!"

"Oh no!" said Miss Tracey. "Stay there, Griff!" And she hurried away.

"Griff! Come out, quickly!" It was Todd.

Griff opened the door. "What's *she* doing in the *boys'* toilets?" he said, pointing at Constance.

"Finding you, of course!" said Constance. "Listen, there's an old hamster cage in the activities room."

"So Hexxa could stay there for today," said Todd.

Griff beamed. "Brilliant!" he said.

"Come on, Hexxa," said Constance. "You're going to a nice safe place. But you have to be very good and quiet." Gently, she picked up Hexxa, stuffed her under her sweatshirt and ran off.

"But what about the police officer?" asked Griff.

"Sssh! Someone's coming!" said Todd. Both boys shot into cubicles and locked the doors.

"Griff?" said Miss Tracey. "How are you feeling?"

"A bit better," said Griff.

"Splendid!" said Miss Tracey. "Come along then!"

Moments later, Griff was standing in front of Mrs Herbert and PC Ahmad, in Mrs Herbert's office. Griff's legs were shaking but he explained about the butcher and the broom. He didn't mention Hexxa!

"Well, Griff," said Mrs Herbert. "This sounds *most* upsetting! The butcher could have really hurt you!"

"Oh no," said Griff. "He wasn't trying to hit *me*! It was this nasty great crow! I was trying to frighten it away!"

Just then, there was a blood-curdling scream.

"What on earth was that?" said Mrs Herbert.

"We'd better find out!" said PC Ahmad. "Come on!"

They all rushed out of the room.

"Stop running, Griff Griffiths!" shrieked the school secretary.

But Griff raced ahead of Mrs Herbert and PC Ahmad and burst into the activities room. The door of the hamster cage was wide open. Hexxa was dive-bombing Miss Tracey!

"This is fun!" Hexxa squawked. Miss Tracey fainted.

"Constance told you to be quiet and good!" Griff hissed.

"But I'm hungry!" complained Hexxa.

Griff thought fast. He opened a window. "Quick!" he said. "Fly outside and hide!"

"Hide?" said Hexxa. "Why?"

"Don't argue – just do it!" growled Griff. "Out!"

He watched Hexxa fly away and then hurried over to Miss Tracey. "It's OK now, Miss Tracey," he said. "Wake up!"

Mrs Herbert stormed in, followed by PC Ahmad.

"There was this horrible big bird," gasped Miss Tracey. "It had huge talons and a nasty beak. And then it spoke!"

"There, there," said Mrs Herbert. "It's the shock."

"Well," said PC Ahmad, "it's obviously a very dangerous bird. We will have to catch it!"

Griff gulped.

"Where did it go, Griff?" Mrs Herbert demanded.

"Err ... I didn't see!" said Griff. "It went so fast!"

He felt sick. What would the police do with Hexxa if they caught her? He had to find her – fast! She was very annoying but she was also very, very special!

"Go back to class, Griff," said Mrs Herbert. "I'll speak to you later!"

"Yes, Mrs Herbert!" said Griff. He ran down the corridor and crashed into the school secretary.

"Griff Griffiths!" she screamed. "For the last time, stop running!"

"Sorry!" he shouted and bolted into the boys' toilets. He needed a place to think.

Chapter 4
Where Is Hexxa?

Griff had a problem. If he tried walking out of the main entrance, the school secretary would see him. All the other doors had security codes and only the teachers knew them. He looked up at the toilet window. It was very small but maybe he could squeeze through?

Griff scrambled on to the toilet seat and opened the window. He hauled himself up, over the metal frame.

"Ouch!" he thought. It really hurt! And he was stuck! All he could do was squirm! He felt as if he was being sawn in two!

"Griff! Why are you up there?"

Griff looked down. It was Constance, standing outside in the playground.

"Great!" thought Griff. "Her again. And how did she get out anyway?"

"I'm trying to find Hexxa!" he growled. "I made her fly out of the window when Miss Tracey fainted."

"Gosh – do you need some help?"

"Yes please! I'm stuck. And if I get unstuck I'll fall flat on my face!

"You're not very high up," said Constance. "You could fall into a wheelie bin. The one for paper and cardboard. I'll get it."

"OK," said Griff. He didn't like the idea but he had no choice.

The wheelie bin was massive and Constance looked tiny beside it but, with a fierce roar, she shoved hard. The bin shot across the concrete and stopped underneath Griff.

"The lid!" cried Griff. "It's shut! And you're too short to open it!"

But Constance was stacking up empty milk crates beside the bin.

"No problem," she said. She scrambled up the crates and flung open the lid. "Now dive!" she said.

"I don't think I can!" moaned Griff.

"You have to!" said Constance. "Listen!"

They could hear Mrs Herbert's voice coming closer.

"Dive!" hissed Constance. "Now!"

Griff looked down into the wheelie bin. He was terrified. But he gave a huge wriggle and suddenly—

"Oof!"

He crash-landed in the bin! The lid fell shut. Bang!

"Oh help!" Griff thought. "Now what?"

"Constance Amelia Grisold!" he heard Mrs Herbert saying. "What are you doing out here?"

"I finished my Maths quickly so I asked my teacher if I could pick up litter," said Constance sweetly. "My after-school club is doing a Clean-Up Challenge."

Griff's jaw dropped. So that was how she'd managed to get past the secretary and out of school! Why hadn't he thought of something like that?

"Splendid, Constance," said Mrs Herbert, "but right now, please go inside."

"But I haven't finished!" Constance complained.

"Don't argue, Constance!" said Mrs Herbert. "Off you go! PC Ahmad needs to look for that bird."

"Still no sign of it," said PC Ahmad.

"No, indeed," said Mrs Herbert, sounding worried.

Crouched among the card and paper, Griff heard them walking away. "Think!" he told himself. "Fast! How are you going to get out of the bin?"

Yes! He'd got it! He started to screw up paper and card to make a pile in a corner that he could climb up. Soon, he'd made a big heap. Then he scrambled up, pushed open the lid and hauled himself over the side.

Oh no! Mrs Dobson, the cook, was staring at him out of the kitchen window!

He ducked down behind the bin but he knew Mrs Dobson had seen him. How long would it take her to raise the alarm? There was no time to lose. Keeping low, Griff scurried across the playground.

"Hexxa!" he shouted urgently. "Hexxa! The police are going to catch you!"

A police van drove through the school gates. Griff could hear dogs barking.

"Hexxa!" he shouted desperately. "The police have got dogs!" He scanned the trees. Where could she be?

Then he noticed the school weather vane. It looked strangely bumpy. Griff waved frantically. Hexxa zoomed down!

"You left me!" Hexxa squawked. "Bad boy!"

"Sssh!" hissed Griff. "I had to. And then you attacked Miss Tracey!"

"I was hungry!"

"Don't start that!" snapped Griff. "Quick! We have to go!"

Griff tried to stuff Hexxa into his pocket.
"What?" he said. "Why won't you fit in?"

"Stop it," squealed Hexxa. "You're hurting me!"

Griff sat Hexxa on his hand and looked at her. "You've grown!" he said in horror. "Quick! Get under my sweatshirt!"

At that very moment, the school fire alarm went off.

"Hexxa?" said Griff. "Is that something to do with you?"

"What?" croaked Hexxa.

"Oh, nothing!" Griff said. He shot out of the side gate and ran off down the road.

Chapter 5
Poor Mrs Herbert!

Back in school, the children were very excited by the fire alarm. They all filed out into the playground and lined up in their classes.

"Well done, everyone!" said Mrs Herbert. "But it turns out it was a false alarm. Go back to your classrooms – quickly!"

Todd saw that Constance was standing on her own next to Mrs Herbert. He stopped and knelt down near her as if his shoe had come undone. "Do you know where Griff is?" he muttered.

"I think he's escaped with Hexxa," Constance hissed. "We need another distraction so no one notices. I set the fire alarm off so it's your turn!"

"OK," said Todd. "Leave it to me!" He stood up. Now what? He had no idea what to do!

"I could smell burning!" Constance explained to Mrs Herbert. "And I thought I could see smoke!"

"It was just some onions frying while I phoned the office!" protested Mrs Dobson, the cook. "Griff Griffiths was climbing out of the wheelie bin! I had to report it, didn't I?"

"Yes, of course, Mrs Dobson," said Mrs Herbert. "It's just a pity you left the onions cooking."

"Shouldn't I have pressed the alarm?" asked Constance, looking innocent.

"Of course you should, dear," said Mrs Herbert. "Better a false alarm than the school burns down. Now back to your lessons, please."

"But Mrs Herbert, what about Griff Griffiths?" demanded Mrs Dobson.

"Yes, Mrs Dobson, I heard you," said Mrs Herbert. "I will check where he is myself. Now please go back to the kitchen and be more careful in future!"

Constance quietly followed Mrs Dobson. Then she skipped off down the corridor. What a bit of luck that she'd smelled those onions! She just hoped Todd could cover for Griff.

"Constance Amelia Grisold!" shouted the school secretary. "Stop skipping!"

Todd's class was nearly back at their classroom when Todd finally had an idea. He hung back and, when his class had turned the corner, he sprinted down to the activities room. He crept over to the cage where the pet mice lived. Carefully, he scooped one out. Then he ran to the school office, opened the door very quietly and put it on the floor.

"Griff's gone home sick," he told his teacher, back at his classroom. "The school secretary told me to tell you." He'd never lied to a teacher before! But he had to do something to help Griff and Hexxa!

In her office, Mrs Herbert felt as if she would like to lie down with a wet towel over her face. The police had gone. There was no sign of the strange bird that had attacked poor Miss Tracey.

Could Griff Griffiths really have been climbing out of a wheelie bin? It made no sense. But why would Mrs Dobson make it up? She really must go and check.

At that very moment, there was a blood-curdling scream.

"Not again!" thought Mrs Herbert. She ran into the school office.

"A mouse! A mouse!" yelled the school secretary. Mrs Herbert fainted.

Chapter 6
Poor Smudge!

Griff ran all the way home. He couldn't think where else to go. He let himself in and collapsed on the sofa.

Hexxa stuck her head out of his sweatshirt.

"I'm hungry," she said. "And I'm squashed in here."

"Yikes," thought Griff. "I look like I've got a football up my jumper!" There was no doubt about it. Hexxa was growing fast. How could he keep her a secret?

Hexxa clawed her way out and stood on his knee.

"Oof!" Griff wished her talons didn't dig in so much.

"I'm hungry," she said again, crossly. Suddenly, there was a loud hiss. A black streak of fur hurled itself at Hexxa. It was Smudge, Griff's cat.

Griff couldn't believe it. Smudge never

hissed – he only purred!

But not any more! Smudge had turned into a killer cat! And Hexxa was fighting back!

Rip! Hexxa's talon tore one of the cushions. Feathers danced in the air.

"I've got to do something – fast!" thought Griff.

A vase of flowers stood on the table. Griff snatched it up and emptied it all over Hexxa and Smudge – and the sofa!

Smudge yowled and jumped back. Hexxa zoomed straight up to the ceiling and perched on the lamp, shrieking. Then the doorbell rang!

Griff froze. Who could that be? It might be someone who knew he should be at school! He tiptoed into the hall, wondering what to do.

Then the letterbox rattled and Todd shouted through it. "Griff! It's us! Let us in!"

"Come in – quickly!" Griff gasped, opening the door. "Smudge attacked Hexxa!"

"Nasty cat," squawked Hexxa. "I hate that cat!" She jumped around, making the lamp swing.

"It's OK, Hexxa," said Griff. "Smudge has gone!"

Constance glared up at Hexxa. "Bad girl!" she said. "We're trying to help you and you're nothing but trouble! Now stay still – you might break the lamp!"

"I don't like you any more," said Hexxa. And she tucked her head under her wing crossly.

Chapter 7
Griff Has Had Enough

"Quickly!" said Constance. "We need a vacuum cleaner and a hairdryer!"

"What's the hairdryer for?" asked Griff.

"To dry out the sofa, of course! We'll vacuum up the feathers and turn over the cushions. Come on!"

As fast as they could, the children cleared up. Griff was still blasting the sofa with the hairdryer when a car drew up outside.

"Uh-oh," said Griff. "It's Mum!"

"We need to go!" said Todd.

"But how are we going to get Hexxa off the lamp?" demanded Griff.

"Kneel down, Griff!" said Constance. "Now!"

"What?" said Griff.

"You heard! I do circus skills."

Griff knelt down. Carefully, Constance climbed on to his shoulders.

"Hold me steady, Todd!" she said.
"I'm going to grab Hexxa! Don't move!"

Griff screwed up his face.
"Concentrate," he told himself. "Just
stay still!"

"Got her!" said Constance, and
jumped down.

They could hear the key in the door.

"Quick! Out the back!" said Griff.

They raced around the side of the house and on to the street.

"Now what?" Todd panted.

"I'm hungry," squawked Hexxa, at once.

Suddenly, Griff had had enough. It was all too much! How could a baby griffin be so much trouble – and *always* hungry? He grabbed Hexxa and plonked her down on the pavement.

"Goodbye, Hexxa," he said, walking back towards his house. "Good luck. Come on, you two!"

"What?" said Constance.

"She's too much trouble," said Griff. "Come on, Todd!"

Todd looked unsure but he followed Griff.

"You can't leave her!" Constance said. "She's a baby! And the police might catch her!"

"Just watch me!" Griff snarled.

"You wimp!" shouted Constance. She scooped up Hexxa. "Come on, Hexxa," she said. "I'll take you to my granny's. She'll know what to do." Then she ran off in the opposite direction.

"Let's go to your house, Todd," said Griff. He was worried about his mum finding the cushion and the damp sofa.

But the further he walked, the sadder he felt. Hexxa had hatched out in *his* hand, from an egg from *his* henhouse, in *his* garden. Griff's eyes began to prickle. It wasn't fair. He'd done his very best to help Hexxa but she was so difficult!

He stood still. "I want Hexxa back," he said.

"I *knew* you'd change your mind," groaned Todd. "And now we've no idea where Constance has gone! Are you really *sure* you want Hexxa back?"

"Of course I want her back!" said Griff. "She's amazing!"

Todd sighed. "She's getting bigger, Griff. What are you going to do with her?"

"I don't know," admitted Griff. "But I can't just give up. Hexxa is *my* griffin!"

"OK," said Todd. "Well, Constance said she was taking her to her granny. But we don't know her granny's name or *anything*!"

Griff's mouth fell open. "Todd, you're a genius!" he shouted. He slapped him on his back. "Constance Amelia *Grisold*! I bet anything her granny is Granny *Gristle*! Come on – let's go!"

Chapter 8
Granny Gristle

All the local kids knew Granny Gristle. She lived in a large, shabby house, hidden from the road by yew trees. She had very long silver hair in a plait. When she went shopping, she rode a big tricycle and wore a long cape. Her dog, Macduff, looked like a wolf!

Griff and Todd peered through the rusty gates. The porch was covered in creeper. Ivy clung to the brickwork and weeds grew out of the cracked front steps.

What if Griff had got it wrong? What if Granny Gristle wasn't Constance's granny?

"After you!" said Todd.

Griff gulped. "OK, follow me," he said.

Together, they crept up to the front door.

"Now or never," said Griff, and he lifted the knocker.

They waited and then, slowly, the door opened. Griff inched closer to Todd.

"You two!" said Constance Amelia Grisold.

Hexxa was sitting on Constance's shoulder. "Go away!" she said to Griff. "I don't like you any more."

"Charming," muttered Griff.

"May we come in?" asked Todd bravely.

"Not if Griff is going to be mean," said Constance.

"Mean?" gasped Griff. "After all I've done!"

"Now then, Constance!" It was Granny Gristle. "Come along in, boys," she said. "We need to sort this out."

"Err … my mum might be wondering where I am," Griff said.

"Well, phone her and say you're with Dr Grisold," said Granny Gristle.

"You're a doctor?" said Griff, looking startled.

"I most certainly am, Griff Griffiths!" said Granny Gristle. "I saved your mother's life when she had measles! So she knows who I am!"

"Wow!" said Todd, his eyes round.

Granny Gristle laughed. "I can see that surprises you both! Now, are you coming in or not?"

In the kitchen, Macduff lay snoozing on the rug. Granny Gristle gave them all mugs of strong tea and huge slices of chocolate cake – all except Hexxa.

"Griffins must only eat fresh meat," said Granny Gristle and put a small plate of raw chicken in front of Hexxa.

"Yummy!" squawked Hexxa and gobbled it up. "More!" She banged her talon on the table.

"Certainly not," said Granny Gristle. "Not till supper-time. And if you behave like that, there won't be any more at all!"

Hexxa glared at Granny Gristle. "I could scratch you with my talons," she said.

"You could try," said Granny Gristle. "But Macduff might not like it."

Macduff opened an eye. He let out a growl that made Griff shiver. Hexxa jumped back.

"Bad diet," said Granny Gristle. "That's what's gone wrong with Hexxa. Constance says she gave her a sandwich. Awful! You have to be so careful with griffins."

Todd and Griff stared at her. "How do you know?" asked Griff.

"Oh, griffins turn up from time to time. Of course, most people think they're dreaming. But this is the first time I've come across a baby."

"I am not a baby," snorted Hexxa. "I'm growing up fast."

"Very fast," smiled Granny Gristle.

"So can she stay with you, Granny?" asked Constance.

"Of course," said Granny Gristle.

"But," said Griff, "but … I wanted her to be my pet."

"Your *pet*?" exploded Hexxa. "No way!"

"I rescued you from the butcher!" said Griff furiously. "And the police! You are *so* ungrateful!"

"Griff," said Granny Gristle. "A griffin can't be a pet. But that doesn't mean you can't visit Hexxa."

"What if she keeps on growing?" asked

Griff. "She could take over the world!"

"Diet," said Granny Gristle, briskly. "Only raw meat. Then I don't think she'll grow much bigger. And she'll behave better."

"I think I must be dreaming," said Todd.

"No, you're not," said Hexxa, and she jabbed him with her beak.

"Stop that!" said Granny Gristle. "If you're living with me, you have to behave, Hexxa."

"I think it'll be great!" said Constance. "Don't you, Griff?"

Griff hesitated. He was still cross with Constance.

"I guess there isn't much choice," he said.

"You can come over whenever you want," said Granny Gristle.

"Let's ask Hexxa," said Griff. He stroked the back of her neck.

"Mmmm," she said. "That's better."

"Hexxa, would you like to live with Constance's granny?" he asked.

Hexxa cocked her head on one side. "Will you come to see me?" she asked.

Griff had a lump in his throat. "Yes," he said. "Of course I will."

"Will there be MEAT?" asked Hexxa.

"Yes," said Granny Gristle. "*Just* meat. But you'll have to behave very well."

"I *do* behave very well," said Hexxa, looking smug. "What are you all laughing at?"

"Oh Hexxa," said Griff. "I'm so glad I found you!"

And everyone else agreed.

About the author

When my younger son was little, he spent most of his life with a little model of Peter Pan from the film *Hook* in his hand. Together they had heaps of adventures. My eldest son enjoyed myths and legends. Somehow my mind put the two together and came up with the idea of a boy who finds a hand-sized griffin – and what might happen next!

This story has been such fun to write! All the characters make me chuckle. I hope you enjoy them too!